Interactive Press

A Hint of Rosemary

Hazel Hall is an Australian poet and musicologist who works across a wide range of poetic forms. She holds a PhD in Education from Monash University. From 2012 to 2018, Hazel was founder and convenor of the School of Music Poets, ACT: an ekphrastic group that collaborated with musicians, song writers, and artists to produce a series of poetry chapbooks. She directed the monthly event Poetry at Manning Clark House in Canberrra from 2018 to 2022. Hazel's work can be found in a wide range of local and overseas anthologies and journals and has been a featured poet in printed journals, on websites and blogs. She has won a number of prizes and editors' awards, and her work has been peer selected three times for the *Red Moon Anthology*. Hazel co-edited *Flood Fire and Drought*; *One Last Border*, *Silver Fugue*, collected works of the School of Music Poets; and *The Ink Sinks Deeper*. Her own collections include *eggshell sky* with calligraphers Angela Hillier, Narelle Jones and Parkinsons artists; *Step by Step* with tai chi practitioner Angelina Egan and *Moonlight over the Siding*, featuring artwork by the late Robert Tingey. Her chapbook *Severed Web*, with artist Deborah Faeyrglenn, highlights environment and climate change. Hazel's crown of sonnets *Please Add Your Signature and Date it Here* is a radio play exploring problems in aged care. *Breathe In, Breathe Out* is a chapbook of haiku linked with answering tanka and cherita. Also due in 2024, with poet Moya Pacey and artist Leena Clark is *Featherfall*, a collection of poems exploring human relationships with birds. In 2024, Hazel will judge her fourth international contest, which to date have included the Tanka Society of America's Sanford Goldstein Contest (2019) , the Haiku Poets of North America's Tanka Contest (2021) and the British Haiku Society's Tanka Contest (2023).

iP

Brisbane

A Hint of Rosemary

a sprig
of rosemary secured
with a safety pin
box gums' guard of honour
down the long bush track

Hazel Hall

Interactive Press
an imprint of IP (Interactive Publications Pty Ltd)
Treetop Studio • 9 Kuhler Court
Carindale, Queensland, Australia 4152
sales@ipoz.biz
http://ipoz.biz/

Printed in 12 pt Adobe Caslon Pro on 14 pt Avenir Book.

ISBN: 978192830722 (PB); 978192830739 (eBk)

Acknowledgements

Poems from this collection have been recorded/published in *Artsound FM*, (2021-2024), *The Canberra Times Panorama* (2020, 2022), *Blithe Spirit* (2023), *Burrow*, (2021, 2022), *Catttails* (2017), 'Fujisan Taiso' *Grieve* (2021), *Kokako* (2022), *Messages from the Embers* (2020), *Milestones* (2021), *MacQueen's Quinterly* (2022- 2024), *Not Very Quiet* (2021), *Moonlight over the Siding* (2018), *Poetry d'Amour* (2021), *Quadrant* (2019, 2022), *Stardust Haiku* (2018-2019), *Sugar Loaf and Humming Birds* (2014), *Temple* (2021), *These Strange Outcrops* (2020) and *Whispering Willows: Tree Poems,* 2022. 'Costco is Selling Coffins' was solicited for Judith Clingan's music theatre *The Threshold* and first performed on 4 March 2023. Many other poems morphed from work published in chapbooks and newsletters. I thank all editors who accepted my work. 'Another Garden' is a response to Marina Tsvetaeva's classic poem 'Sad.' Thanks to Subhash Jaireth for publishing my original translation in *Axon*. For further information on individual poems please refer to *Notes*.

I am deeply grateful to Geoff Page OAM, who assessed and edited the manuscript in its early and final stages. My gratitude also to Suzanne Edgar who assessed and edited the original manuscript, Kathy Kituai who read and edited both original and final drafts, Carmel Summers who proofed and assessed the final draft and Dr Mark O'Connor OAM who also assessed the manuscript. Without the valuable editorial support and advice from these four poets, this collection would not have gone to print. Strathnairn Poets Kerrie Nelson, Rosa O'Kane, Moya Pacey, Sue Peachey and Sandra Renew also provided much appreciated feedback on various poems. Thanks also to Rohan Beuttel, Tony Williams and the Tram Stop Poets, who offered feedback on some of the poems. To Peter Monaghan, my gratitude for including poems from this collection on *Artsound FM*. I am indebted to Subhash Jaireth for his translation workshops, to Professor Marianne Boruch for introducing me to Ellen Bryant Voigt's book of sonnets *Kyrie*, to Professor Daniel Metraux, for sharing insights from documents owned by his late mother. I am deeply grateful to all the editors of anthologies and journals who have accepted my work.' Dr David Reiter, my wonderful publisher, sincere thanks. Lastly, to my husband Dr Christopher Dorman, for his technical assistance, proofreading and unfailing support, my love and deepest appreciation.

Praise for *A Hint of Rosemary*

Hazel Hall is a lover of music as well as words. Her poems tend towards the quality of song, and she speaks of the musicologist George List telling her how 'only stability of intonation distinguishes song from speech.' Many of her poems seek music that may 'with its art, discover or retrace / the sacredness, until it finds a place / within— that prize, that dazzling secret bit / of heaven, when we make meaning out of it.' Although all of her poems are derived from sonnets, they display Hazel's interest in poetic and musical forms in a wonderful range of topics. Unpretentious yet potent descriptions and evocations abound. They can be as simple and haiku-like as this: 'Two magpies on a fence were swapping notes, / swallows were preparing to take leave. / Lorikeets with sapphire-coloured throats / swung on a willow's long kimono sleeves'.

Each poem finds a different way to touch the heart. 'Shadow at the Wheel' depicts the nightmares of, one suspects, a woman who has fled an abusive lover: 'I listen, praying not to hear that sound / the dark car humming as it cruises past / headlights dipped, a shadow at the wheel / daring me to peek into the street.' That 'black sedan' might grow to rival 'the black dog' as a proverbial phrase.

Harsh times and choices are recalled in "Returned Soldier 1947" when a veteran is offered, for PTSD, a generous choice of the best modern remedies: insulin, electro-shock or lobotomy: 'So think about it soldier, chat it over with your wife / and let us have your answer in a day or so.'

If you are tired of "the talented ear-ache of modern poetry", of poems that seem written less to touch the reader than to show the poet's cleverness, you will warm to Hazel Hall's work. Her poems are about real identifiable events, and she has real and important things to say about each of them.

– **Dr Mark O'Connor OAM**, Olympic Laureate, Enviromentalist and Shakespeare Scholar, and author of *The Olive Tree*.

In this exploration of the many forms that a modern sonnet can take, in *A Hint of Rosemary,* Hazel Hall displays her mastery of Petrarchan, Shakespearean and hybrid sonnets in her engagement with people, nature, social issues and the past. From the Kongouru first painted by George Stubbs to the ill-fated Robert Scott, from John Keats to an unmarked child's grave at Wallendbeen, each subject is marked by Hall's acute perception and awareness of the world in all its layers and inherent musicality. Her proficiency with Japanese forms is also evident in both the haiku which subtly subtitle each section in this book and in their integration within the sonnet form. This experimentation ranges from a sonnet written in haiku to the adaptation of the sonnet form to haibun. As Hall admits, one must follow a recipe first before experimenting. Hall succeeds in both. *A Hint of Rosemary* is a book that both obeys and challenges the conventions of the English sonnet, while dealing with the ordinary and the extraordinary.

– Carmel Summers, author of *Lost in the Pleiades*

According to Beethoven, once you know the rules, you can break them. When it comes to traditional end-lines, octave, sestet and pentameter in a sonnet, Hazel Hall is well practiced. However, her unrhymed experimental free-verse, haibun as sonnets, along with combinations of other Japanese genres like tanka in this collection, not only give credence to Beethoven's affirmation. We are offered exciting possibilities of just what today's sonnet can be, like two poems spliced into one yet still readable as two (rhyming patterns intact). A sonnet is offered as concrete poetry. There are letters to loved ones— Captain Scott, for instance, pens a letter to his widow. Hazel's history and memoir is insightful and often playful, as she imaginatively thrusts the reader into a whirlwind of 'remember-when'.

– Kathy Kituai, poet, teacher and diarist, author of *The Art of Catching Jam Before it Burns*

Contents

Hard Lessons

old photos
just for a moment
the scent of hay

A River Crossed

1.

You told me of a tin your father kept,
filled with images you recollect
of country life. His lineage retraced
in miscellaneous articles he placed
inside. The lid revealed a traveling scene
depicting harsher times when life was lean
encaptioned: *Journey to Prosperity.*
Your heart lay in that faded century
and leathery man who drove his herd across
the Murrumbidgee while the torrents tossed
his beasts across the lather of the floods.
Sweat of horse and man, the stench of mud
as cattle clambered up the umber banks
bellowing, with leeches on their flanks.

2.

Gone thirty years ago. They could be days
He's with you still. The dead run through our veins,
and little things connected with him sought
while the loss was foremost in your thoughts.
The land went to his boys; the house consigned
to you. One day a brother came to find
that tin of tokens sitting on its shelf—
worth more to all of you than family wealth.
A violent storm broke out when he ransacked
your ties and trust. That one outrageous act
split the bond—a mighty river crossed,
neither sibling knowing what was lost
until you saw that all those angry rants
were only leeches on the cattle's flanks.

Hindsight

My tiny son is in his cowboy vest.
A birthday present. Doesn't he look cute?
Sheriff's badge pinned on his little chest,
two holsters at the hips to fire six-shoots.
Dad, obsessed with costumes of the past,
took the shot and made the print with care.
His negatives, hung in the dark room, cast
shadows on my face while dangling there.
Divisions that I scarcely realised
imprinted on the paper of my mind
developed over years, had grown and thrived.
I woke too late.
      Now suddenly I find
my *mea culpa* loaded in the toys
given by another little boy.

Big Leg

You sent an image of your newborn son.
One tiny limb. The caption read: *Big Leg*.
Perfect and pink, on a freshly ironed sheet
as he lay sleeping in his bedside cot.
Stubborn. He'd already kicked his mum,
created pain and caused a watershed,
let out a mighty cry, and grabbed the teat
informing everybody who was boss.

His little limbs will crawl and walk and run,
and in the drowsy dawns, bounce on your bed.
As time strides by and memory retreats
we'll find this photo in a secret spot.
Hey, see what I turned up. Who would have thought?
Look what his bragging father's camera caught.

Boundaries

1.

We had a tangled mass of poles and wire
looped to a pylon, hard to extricate.
We'd dodge the furrows made by muddy tyres,
to wrestle with the timber's heavy weight
the way I did when only just a child
and kids were ordered to cooperate.
If I had taken trouble to inquire
my uncle might have said: *A gate's a gate.*
Now time has come for memories to retire.
Those poles will warm our winter on a late
August afternoon, when coals inspire
yarns to garnish T-bones on our plates.
A hook-up to the future's been acquired—
replacement easier to operate.

2.

Our weathered fence, saw-edged and sunlit-speckled
where birds leave messages in paint-tube dribbles,
has drop-in space that welcomes in odd creatures
with squeeze-through chook holes scratched by busy feet.
It offers gaze-and-wonder gaps for children
and room for rhythms made with brittle sticks.
Between its posts, a story-telling library
conjures up strange fantasies from shadows.
Yet solemn. Tuned for evening reflections,
it keeps its dignity. Age peeks through timber.
A memory-fence with family connections,
it often speaks in little creaks and whispers.
Don't-fence-me-in planks borrowed from a song—
how can they be replaced with Colourbond?

all souls' day

yesterday's giants silent silos in the mist
waterlogged from the creek bed frog song
remembering that steamy evening cup of tea
just a year since she left the pantry bare
first day of term payment owing on their books
one little tortoise tries to run the school bus
controlled burn for a moment the scent of fear
set in stone loss too much to comprehend

silhouettes at evening's edge a man and dog
setting sun sulphur screeches split the sky
knock off time a cold one waiting at the pub
feral kittens squeaking in the milking shed
jack o' lantern shadows dangle in the trees
all souls' day too many memories

Absence Does Not Make the Heart Grow Stronger

for Kate

You abandoned me for a vacation
in another state for five long days
while I was relocated with a minder
and forced to share her attention with a dog.
On your return, I rushed to greet my keeper,
wove two figure eights around her ankles,
granted her the luxury of a cuddle,
and even purred in sheer duplicity.
Then tentatively tiptoed for your greeting
with studied nuzzle, but just for a moment.
When you picked me up, I clawed and struggled.
First some retribution must take place.
Hurt is hurt, and you must suffer longer.
Absence does not make the heart grow stronger.

Shadow at the Wheel

Secure the doors. Slip window locks in place.
Put mobile phone beside the bed before
the lights go out. Not one lamp in the hall
betrays the hour. Breathe deeply. Settle down.
Check the curtains. Look beneath the bed.
Turn the doona. Watch the cat hook pleats
into the fabric.
       Will it ever stop?
Lurking in my sleep throughout the night,
I listen, praying not to hear that sound—
the dark car humming as it cruises past
headlights dipped, a shadow at the wheel
daring me to peek into the street.
Three times I've moved house. Each time I learn
to hope and then the black sedan returns.

The Miner's Wife

Kadina Cemetery, 2016

home to gravel, ants and little shells
        not one hint of green peeps through the stones
summer beats its harsh relentless drum,
        winter lends a cloak of bitter cold
rains drip over stories no one tells
        around this lonely plot that history owns
two lie resting in a place for one
        a boy aged twelve, the girl not two years old
nothing in the records that can tell
        and so the breezes blow bleak overtones
perhaps some stories cannot be expunged
        in this town of shafts, above the toll
all-abiding— Wesley Chapel bells
        grief is an organ— and its bellows swell

    old mine shaft
    gilded with sunlight
    at day's end
    a pair of canaries
    twitter overhead

The Yellow Line

in dreams i see the yellow line
time after time—i cower behind
this stripe before a steep decline
the station scene fixed in my mind

      lights that blind—the siren's whine
      i stand beside her—wonder why
      she frees the hand that's held in mine
      and dives across the yellow line

screech of brakes—the steel wheels grind
a final hiss from the other side
i try to run away and hide
is silence yellow?—i can't decide

then men jump over the warning sign
STAND BACK! they cry—***BEHIND THE LINE!***

Kyrie

in response to Ellen Bryant Voigt

Hard to think you didn't predict this time
in ninety-five when you wrote *Kyrie*,
investigation of the curse that spread
like anarchy, and claimed to be from Spain.
You wrote despair, you wrote unanswered prayers
stench of flesh, small boxes lined in white,
and wagon loads compassion could not pass.
In this new pandemic, retrospect
must not interfere with politics.
The world's a virus, crammed with tweets and waves,
prevarications floating on a cloud
of economics. When to intervene
and ventilate? Silently the aged,
homeless and impaired begin to fade
back into your pages
                    Kyrie

The Cost

He wore a tee and cap while playing golf.
Sliced the virus with a double cross
that day the rate and numbers climbed too high.
Almost a hundred thousand people lost.
They died alone. No priest to bless their souls,
none to sponge them with a scented cloth
speak softly as each moment bunkered by,
or mourn the silence of a switch turned off.
Funerals sterilized for protocol.
Chairs spaced apart—who could predict the cost
or gather solace from those brief goodbyes?
We grieved for the bereaved ones as we watched
that fairway clip where he was playing golf.
Around his neck he wore an albatross.

Morning Coffee

Covid pandemic, 2020

Each morning I see the man at end of our street
sitting inside the garage that's under his house.
There, he's arranged a table and two plastic chairs.
Behind them a curtain is hanging that once was a sheet.
Three cups have been placed on his table under the house
where he sits with his wife and a neighbour, discussing the
news.
Grins and raises a hand when I pass in the car,
while I wonder what hides beyond that mysterious sheet.

Maybe his tools are kept there, sorted and stacked
as neat as this little cafe under the house.
Or perhaps there is nothing important, simply a mess
left on his agenda's back-burner, day after day.
For he knows that all menial labour must take second
place
when there's a neighbour to talk to and coffee to taste.

      tucking themselves
      inside their bubble
      second wave

Costco is Selling Coffins

Costco is selling coffins and urns. Don't stress.
Death's affordable. That brings relief
to families hard pressed to find the cash
when every cost is finally revealed.
I've checked the range and think I might accept
in readiness for when the Reaper creeps
behind me suddenly and in a flash
makes a grab. Too late when fate is sealed.

Come and join me in a spending fest
on Monday morning, heading the stampede,
plastic ready in our fists. Perhaps
buying in bulk will screw a better deal
for boxes we can store our blankets in
and canisters, for holding vitamins.

Dead Day

Margaret Scott Simmons (1926-2023)

A scented bath awaits with soapy froth
heralding an hour of glorious sloth.
Inspired by an aunt, for sanity.
I live for dead days, she would say to me.
Once I enjoyed these quiet times of zen
until a virus ordered more of them,
so I've set this day aside all to myself,
to further every aspect of my health.

Echoes of past laughter thud like lead;
outside, the street is silent as a stone.
Perhaps I'd better spend the day in bed
leaving a recording on my phone
to say: *The person in this house is dead.*
Hang up—no message needed at the tone.

Plastic Bags

Subsistence is his supermarket bags
beneath the eaves. Not much less when we die.
They're safe enough there. Nobody would try
to steal recycled things. He took his fags.
Last night was minus five. The cold still nags.
While public servants, cozy in high-rise
admired the moonlight, wintry crystals prised
their stinging needles through his pre-owned swag.

Collar over dreadlocks, he zigzags
around well-clad commuters for some fries,
and, if a car collects him, that should buy
some kind of bed. A different time that drags.
I gave him money. All the change I had,
his eyes accused, as biting as the sky.

A Trail of Stars

If I had known, I would have pressured you
to take more care. A pilot of the sky
must be intuitive. Was it the blue
beyond the blue or need to satisfy
a whim? With clock forgotten in your pack
you traced the hills and gullies of your mind
and rode your fear along untraveled tracks.
Was it the Moon or Mars you hoped to find
until a strange and sudden stillness jarred
the frenzy of that afternoon in flight?
You might have heard the hidden choirs of stars
singing like sirens for the coming night.

A thousand aeons in that moment spun.
The blinding light—before the final plunge.

Hard Lessons

As kids, we learned hard lessons from the farm.
Feral kittens in the milking shed
looked so sweet I thought we'd catch one each
and tame it as a pet. We'd chosen names
already. Neil grabbed some hessian sacks
that once held chaff. I found a battered lid
from a milk can. Filled it to the brim
after milking when farm cats were fed.

Neil bagged Spotty. Tried to pull him out.
The kitten hissed and shredded Neil's arm
until released. When grown up, Spotty humped
the house cat, Patches. After she gave birth
to six fine offspring by the kitchen stove,
they vanished and the episode was closed.

I Am Just Going Outside

snow clouds over
the lofty mountain's
tranquility
I hear a thousand cranes
proclaim our urgent need

Dazzled

for Robert Tingey (1940-2017)

were those three men, who faced the infinite
in pounding silence, locked in lunar night
and saw this earth rise like an embryo,
struck with wonder like John Keats, who wrote
of Chapman's Homer as he realized
that poetry can take us to the skies?

were you also dazzled on the day
when screaming seagulls carried time away
across the glaciers of glistening glass
that reached to pull your fingers in their grasp
through landscape so ethereal, and still
it mesmerized your spirit with its will,
calling at your bedside now and then—
was that what rose before you at the end?

Rucksack

for Christopher

This canvas rucksack from an era gone,
is vintage '71, honest and strong;
the dog chain of your caution on its frame
with padlock battered from the baggage claim.

Rough times, it's seen. Slit lengthwise in Peru,
thrown on a smuggler's train, soaked on a roof,
Nothing can replace what it withstood—
I'd sprinkle it with stardust if I could.

Reluctantly, you've bought a trolley bag
which won't need hoisting on a tired back,
but keep the battered relic with great pride
and boast of family travels packed inside.
Courted by cobwebs, here the old sack sits
waiting for its owner's final trip.

Storm in Phnom Penh

With roll of drums and cymbol clash, the storm
hits our stilt house lodge with mighty force.
We cling together, trying to keep warm
and dodge the deluge. Water takes its course.
The bar performs a sashay. Torrents slide
across the deck upending sodden shades.
Beneath a firmament that's opened wide
another case for progress has been made.

Soon this blue-chip land will be reclaimed
by Government and sold. They'll drain the lake,
bulldoze little businesses. A chain
of hotels will spring up. There's cash at stake.
Cheap labour will be wanted. When in need
one takes what's offered. There are mouths to feed.

The Kongouro from New Holland

Perched upon a rock, you turn to view
Dreamtime origins one final time
at dawn of the invasion of your land.
Perhaps you're sensing chaos yet to come.
Those hills will disappear and buildings sear
the sky to sever freedoms of the past.
White men will place you on their coat of arms
harbinger of the guns that bring you harm.

Painted from sketches and a sibling's skin,
does apprehension glitter in your eye,
point of the artist's focus? Now displayed
in Greenwich London, home is far away.
You're packed there on a supermarket shelf,
emblem of our stewardship and wealth.

Returned Soldier, 1947

in memory of Bill Young

Take your choice of treatments. Mind you, now it's over
we expect young lads like you to shape up quickly.
This malaise of yours is sudden. It's a worry.
Think of your wife and children. Snap out of it for their sake;
If not we have three options here on offer.

Insulin's recommended for those highs and lows
and been the most successful. You'll be pleased
with the speed it takes you back to normal.

If that's not beneficial, we have another option:
electrical convulsions. They should still those violent dreams.
You'll feel a little jolt, then another and you'll be a new man.

If all else fails, we'll try an operation
on your frontal lobes. The cure is guaranteed.

So, think about it soldier, chat it over with your wife
and let us have your answer in a day or so.

The Core of Fall

Ottawa, October 2012; for Marilyn

A crimson maple leaf danced on a pole
in brilliant light above the shaded street
that day when leaves were crisp beneath our feet
rustling little rhythms as we strolled.
I reached across somebody's fence and stole
two chrysanthemums, once perfect blooms
and sampled their distinguishing perfume.
You told me that your friends were growing old.

We breathed the core of Fall into our souls.
　　Floral essence is a state of grace
　　to nurture safely in a sacred place
　　before assailing frosts demand their toll.
Then clouds crept by like grey pashmina folds.
The day began to fade. Our bones were cold.

Noh

after Walter de la Mare

slowly, silently, masked like moons
they walk the night in tabi shoes
across the bridge from the divine
stories threaded in the pine
that stands forever at the back
of centre stage as spotlights catch
men who kneel in neat culottes
and strike the music's paradox

awakening the ghosts still deep
in netherlands' mysterious sleep
released from history—gliding by
visors hiding silver eyes
assuming that we too have been
drifting down their silver stream.

Six Pigs

Nazca, 1985

An image haunts me like a song refrain:
the woman walking down a Cusco lane,
black eyes twinkling from her weathered face,
accepting grunt-work with a cheerful grace.
Child on her back while trying to withstand
the wind, she clutches six leads in her hand.
Trotting at each end I see a pig
though, thankfully for her, they're not too big.

Indulgence is required when walking swine,
reminding me of writing and the times
I put my words on leads and let them walk
allowing me to eavesdrop as they talk,
and I rejoice to feel their steady pull
direct me till your hearts and minds are full.

Hummingbird

Nazca, 1985

A hummingbird darts forth from flower to flower,
smaller than the crimson blooms beneath.
Her bright wings whirr as if they'll never cease
as petals flutter earthward in a shower.
She hovers, bee-like, sampling every treat
while I marvel that this tiny heart,
is able to pulsate ten times as fast
as mine—throughout the summer's stinging heat.

As tourists hover over Nazca's plains
scanning geolyths in dry terrain,
pulses will be racing when they find
the giant bird—drawn in a single line.
Roused by this endangered work of art,
will they fear for its micro counterpart?

Rat

Sumatra, 1983

The Grand Hotel is reeking from decay.
A huge rat waddles past the kitchen door,
large and sleek, with bloated throat and gut
reminding me of leftovers from lunch.
Guests on bamboo couches stretch and yawn,
belch and chat or smoke clove cigarettes.
A stranger passes in the corridor
invades my space and cups me in the crutch.

I turn to stone. He smiles and strolls away.
Now I am running— running from that scum.
My love lies horizontal with a book.
Blame and anger pour like rancid soup.
Me too. The guy felt me too, he remarks.
There'll be a schedule change. Time to depart.

Message to Mama

after the airstrike, 2013

our donkeys wait to take the heavy load
of kindling that we sell at the bazaar
(fear smells of petrol, but it can't be shown
you tell us, Mama—men don't make a fuss)
i'm sure it is the wild birds heading home
the wind is roaring—little brother asks
are they crows? i wish that i could grow
wings like them—now they're surrounding us

in a flash i see the donkeys thrown
through the air—i think they'll hit the stars
then i notice little brother float
for a moment, landing in the dust
and worry what you'll say—we can't come home
'cause now we're nothing—and that isn't much

Squeezed

a room's available   it has your name   tucked in
the wing for disabilities
they know that you avoid the metal frame that might
betray an insecurity
your children took the running   all your things   were
spread out
what to take and what to not   some items claimed by
family
some to bring   a stash on ebay   some for the op shop
there's not much time to view your scraps of life
proudly displayed in their new owners' places
paintings, chairs an antique carving knife
photographs displaying happy faces
they're stored in your recall
this must suffice you're
being squeezed
into decreasing
spaces

Purplue Skies

letter to Fanny Brawne

My Sweetest Girl—
I look forward to advancing health
from our old walks, wrapped in your warm affection
(if there be need that I convince myself).
I tried to find a word for your perfection
but could not choose between purple or blue,
so, in the mixture of the thought, chose purplue
for both of us, a colour from those two.
How sickness keeps dividing me and you!

Pamper me with the tenderness you sealed
so often in the pages of your letters.
Do you hear the thrush sing o'er the field?
Perhaps it is a sign of milder weather.
Sometimes I wish that you too, could be ill...
but only since I crave your loving still.

Ever yours,
my dearest Fanny
JK

Letter to Theo

for my sister Virginia

The evening stunned my senses. Showers of stars
outlined in indigo, as bright as day,
above the Rhône in rose and chartreuse rays
transfixed it with empyrean repertoire.
It must have been quiescence of the Bear
that coaxed me from inside my solitude
into the starscape's strange infinitude
of constellations in the gaslight's glare.

Was it heaven that magnified the spheres,
to drown my stubborn spirit in its light,
releasing myriads of stalactites
into the water? Mute upon the pier
I saw two lovers, blind to all that grace,
so I spilled the stars on canvas. Just in case.

On Driving Down North Jindalee Road

Cootamundra, NSW, 2017

One mellow afternoon I drove alone
after we'd been reading poetry.
Deciding that I'd take the long way home,
I chose the track around North Jindalee.
No other vehicle was on that road
and I could rattle through the gravel, free
to wonder as the sun touched tiny stones
and nuzzled yellow leaves on poplar trees.

Two magpies on a fence were swapping notes,
swallows were preparing to take leave.
Lorikeets with sapphire-coloured throats
swung on a willow's long kimono sleeves.
In that instant sheep wore golden fleece,
then daylight left me wrapped in twilight's peace.

amazing grace—
wayside unveilings
of the divine

Leaving Canberra

in memory of Julia Kaylock

We are leaving Canberra. Going inland, from air that chokes
more than smoke from steam trains of our childhood days
with our travel bags crammed full of items from a list
found on the Emergency Fire Survival Kit.
Families have instructions and boxes of P2 masks
in case the sky swirls quickly into molten gold.
They have hand-written details. Know where to find the key
of our country cottage in case we're on a walk.

The sky will be blue, air clearer. My lungs will cease to sting.
Bees will hover over the calendulas' apothecaries.
I will open the windows, hear magpies' clarinets
and cockatoos' bad language as they prune the trees.
On checking *Fires Near Me* we've found the roads are clear.
Now I feel that I'm deserting everybody here.

To My Widow

letters from Captain Scott to his wife Katherine

March 12, 1912

Darling, I have doubts of pulling through
and take advantage of the warmth to pen
letters preparatory to a close.
The first to you, on whom my purpose clings
awake, asleep—if anything befalls
please understand how much you've meant to me—
I've pleasant memories as I depart.

I shan't have suffered pain, but take my dues
full of vigour. When provisions end
we stop within reach of the next depot.
The cold is biting, sometimes angering
but here again, the hot food drives it forth.
So, you must not imagine tragedy—
take consolation from these facts, dear heart.

March, 1912. Date Unknown.

Since my writing, we have little food or fuel.
Please follow these last wishes with good sense.
Our boy will be your comfort now. I know
the country we have proudly served will bring
all the help you need which I have sought.
I pray the boy will have a fine career
bring good sense to the world and makes his mark.

This piece of Union Jack I leave to you.
Your portrait and the boy's lie in my breast.

If only there were time before I go
to tell you more! But where would one begin?
The cold is piercing. Now my time is short.
When I'm gone, remarry if you please—
'twill ensure our boy continues his good start.

God bless you, my own darling!

Your loving
Robert

I Am Just Going Outside

an imaginary entry from Captain Scott's diary

Ross Shelf, March 28, 1912

As these blackened fingers wrap the pen
a blizzard howls and circles round our tent.
Poor Oates gone in our silence of consent—
gone between the hours of now and then.
Twenty miles to go—I don't know when
you'll read this, darling, for it can't be sent
just yet—that damned crack opens like a vent.
Where are you, Oates? You were the best of men.

Doubt is a dog. It bites then bites again.
We've done our duty and should be content.
I've loved you truly—in the worst event
thoughts of you will warm me at the end.
May God forgive what I did not prevent!
I'm going outside—we all knew what he meant.

A Hint of Rosemary

a glimpse
of the eternal minute
shooting star

Freesias on the Hillside

in memory of Neil Ernest Parkin (1943-2006)

Someone has planted freesias by the trail
to the summit of our hill. They bloom
more profusely since the rains. Perhaps
that is the way of grief—a sudden rush
of childhood memories from the milking shed.
We all chose favourite cows. The faded name
Freesia still remains above the bail
where Neil's special beast would reach to eat.

Decades later, after Neil collapsed
floral perfumes drifted with the hymns.
As we left the church I thought I glimpsed
a boyish image near the entourage.
This flood of amaranthine, gold and white
and heavy scent will wrack my sleep tonight.

On an Unmarked Grave

Wallendbeen, New South Wales, c. 1875

The only resting space I can provide
is in this little plot. The priest is kind.
Overhead, he makes the sacred sign
to intercede with Him, who reigns on high.
Silently, I hold you one last time
beside the earthen cradle where you'll lie
one day after birth, light as a sigh,
my tiny bird—you've fallen from the sky.

White stones will grace your grave. I dab my eyes
with kerchief, for I'm granted but a while;
box gums standing silent by your side,
a gravel quilt to keep you warm and dry.
The woman in the big house, walking by
this quiet place won't stop to wonder why.

      setting sun
      in the daisy's petals
      a prayer

Elegy for Pete

in memory of Ian 'Pete' Griffith (1942-2011)

Death is like a stone thrown in a pond—
rings of ripples radiate beyond
the moment passed until they fade away
and the stone embeds itself in sand and clay
leaving stillness.
               So, it was your turn
to listen to the final sweet nocturne.
It's just a little sojourn here on earth.
Perhaps you thought your struggle wasn't worth
the effort.
        Though you never did believe
in afterworlds, in this life you achieved
enough, inspiring us to carry on,
and, ever since the day we learned you'd gone,
when I hear your name, inside my mind
I see the ripples that you left behind.

Sunday School Picnic

Aspendale, Victoria, 1950

Forty kids in two removal vans
without restraint or evacuation plans
would blithely bump for thirty miles or so
in my childhood, many years ago.
We'd jiggle, giggling at the slightest lurch,
singing choruses we'd learned at church;
sandwiches and cordial in a crate,
parents not expecting us till late.

Arriving, we would tumble wildly out,
each rushing to the water with a shout,
discarded clothing strewn with anxious hands
as eager feet stamped patterns in the sand,
to snatch the bliss of sinking with a sigh
in wallowing waves beneath the shrieking sky.

Words Remembered

Namadji, ACT, July 16, 1969;
for John Saxon and Mike Dinn

It wasn't Parkes, but Honeysuckle Creek
Namadji, where a crew of engineers
tracked those seven minutes on the moon
(the dream-dance in slow-motion on its crust).

Dinn and Saxon, snapped at the console,
have landed on the Aussie dollar coin
to mark the Fiftieth Anniversary
beamed up for politics, yet etched
into former times.
   The cigarette
in one man's hand has disappeared; perhaps
lost in an Orwellian memory hole.
Back at Namadji, six slabs hit the spot.
announcing: *One Small Step, One Giant Leap*—
Armstrong's other words deemed obsolete.

   taking another
   bite of the cherry—
   gibbous moon

Carol of the Mulberry

music after Thomas Tallis

On this southern summer's night
I wrap you in a silken cloth
bequeathed to you by velvet moths
that hover in the fading light.

They gather in the orchard where
the Mulberry tree spreads out its limbs
to join me in a mother's hymn
and bless you in unending prayers.

A cross hangs in the charcoal sky
forewarning that the time is late.
Each hour unravels and escapes;
like moths we live, like moths we die.

Then love awakens from the tomb
and opens like a silk cocoon.
Love awakens from the tomb
and opens like a silk cocoon.

Lux Benigna: Lead Kindly Light

in memory of Ella Hazel Violet Outhred (1917-1993)

When we rehearsed that hymn tune while she slept
with Morpheus, our mother woke and leaped
from sickbed to piano to direct
the singing. She was rarely circumspect.
No—not like that, she cried, *Andante pace!*
and sitting down, expressed the lilting grace
suggestive of an old-time sarabande—
her ghostly partner hovering at hand.

So, we traveled back to childhood days,
clustered round her, singing as she played.
Then in a flash I felt the moment slip
into the tempo of that hymn she picked.
Grief is my mother's music on that night
and I must practice till I have it right.

Soliloquy

Grey shrike thrush, you pipe another song
through the dusk when light has almost gone.
A melody in silver notes that glide
through the air then shimmer and subside.
I listen as they heal my tired mind
with their cleansing message while the wild
grasses swish to rhythms of the wind
offering thanksgiving for your hymn.
Perhaps your music seeks the poet's goal—
to find a way into another soul.
And, with its art, discover or retrace
the sacredness, until it finds a place
within—
        that prize, that dazzling secret bit
of heaven, when we make meaning out of it.

Bethungra Spiral

in memory of Stan Marks

You've always been a railroad man at heart.
We're riding on the Northbound as it winds
up two tunnels, while its counterpart
is moving downhill on the other line.
Picked up the train from Junee at the start,
to catch this lap. I see your spirits climb
as the Southbound rumbles to the past.
Your smiles become a spiral, intertwined
end to end.   The sun is out at last
to warm the future after your decline
slip-sliding downhill till new capsules sparked
a turnaround. The cancer's now confined
to monthly check-ups. Having lost its grip,
today you're celebrating with this trip.

     how long blues—
     a hospital trolley
     rattles

A Potassium Hit's the Thing

A handy snack that fills the hunger gap
produces sounds much sweeter than the rest.
The muse likes comfort food when she's been pressed,
with or without that waxy Santa cap.
Though it comes with the convenience of a wrap
sometimes it squelches into bags or vests.
Stores sell plastic cases. I'll invest
in one, in case of similar mishaps.

Researchers show it's simple to reverse
my stress before performance; reconcile
the panic cycle, calm my frazzled nerves.
A potassium hit's the thing. So, for a while
I'll keep a few placebos in reserve—
Bananas have such reassuring smiles.

Let the Bass Walk With You

Chet Baker in Tokyo, 1987

Your song begins at dusk when the air
is heavy with late day and scented with plums.
Leftover sunbeams kindle aubergine hills.
Pink clouds ripple the river as you slip
through the mysteries of substitute clusters.
Let the bass walk with you on the way.

Glissade into the strangeness of evening.
Stray into purples on the flat side.
Spike your Bb minor with a nine.
Play last wisps of cloud soaking up the bright.
Let the keyboard's tritones wink
when that cymbal moon is brushed
with gold as it climbs through the sky.
Take it easy. Play 'Once long ago'.
Play this drowsy, drowsy night.

> almost blue
> a trickle of claret
> left in my glass

Carpal Trouble

Underneath his palm, a passage hides
to tune the strings and ligaments that serve
his hand, while tendons effortlessly glide
around the arteries and median nerve.
Perhaps no harm will come if he insists
on doggedly repeating that one phrase.
Or does continued pressure on his wrist
torment his hand and sets the nerves ablaze?

Perfection is the Devil's furtive sparks
firing the carpal tunnel ligament.
He feels its needles shimmering like stars,
rinforzandos in consecutive attempts.
One day he'll pack his music up. She'll grieve
to see her best performance student leave.

...and on earth, Peace

the child asleep in a cattle stall
is the child in the belly of a mother
held hostage in a tunnel
the child born in an air raid shelter
the child lost under rubble
and the dead child in a father's arms
who has lost his wife and family
crying *see what they have done*

and there is all of us gazing
at our screens and doing nothing
adorning trees with coloured lights
living the season with bubbles
and hoping that something will be done
by others and peace will come

The Violin Maker

for Christopher

You're in your workshop carving future tunes
from pristine hardwood. Not a chip nor scratch.
Mellow as a golden afternoon
in a forest of Tasmanian Ash
where ancient trunks reach skyward to receive
benedictions from the firmament.
Eisteddfods of tomorrow fill the leaves
until a tree becomes an instrument.

My fingers trace the waist. I gently scroll
around the ribs. Caress the tail piece.
Hear ghostly music from the sounding holes
that resonates with chirruping long ceased.
Tradition has been honoured in the mould
of Stradivari—beauty tooled from grief.

Poems Written on a Scribbly Gum

for Kaleb and Lana

In this image I unearthed today
my grandchildren are rambling in the bush
with hiking staffs discovered on the ground.
I sense the song and rhythm of their walk
in shoes inviting grass to tickle toes;
ants to creep inside and take a bite,
the sun to burn. This wisdom they must learn
from the hieroglyphics of the land.

I hear their chattering as they inspect
tiny flowers and insects in the earth,
see how she clasps her brother's arm to gape
at poems written on a scribbly gum.
The memory crystalises—now I see
the special rock they chose and gave to me.

Another Garden

You'll see the sign that says: *50 Ahead*.
Make your way across the little bridge:
white rails at the side where poplars rise,
new leaves sparkling, filled with silvereyes.
Willows on the banks will dangle green
dreadlocks through their shadows in the stream.

Creaks as iron gates open. Recollect
the scent of fresh-turned earth from long ago
and marble figures staring on the lawns.
Inside an empty chapel, hear a choir's
anthem drifting through the open door.
Notice granite, carefully inscribed.
Around the gravel, grasses will be trimmed—
the gardener likes to exercise his scythe.

A Hint of Rosemary

Washington, D.C., November 22, 1963

A hint of rosemary is in the air
over the unblemished southern lawn
framed by frozen faces at the fence
as if they're waiting for a photo shoot.
The secretary's packed, about to leave
when Bobby, blind-eyed, urgently implores
she view what he cannot.
              She vacillates
beside the box. He hears her stifled cry
to see the ghostly restoration, preened
for last impressions like an effigy
from Madame Tussaud...
            dropping down the lid,
she turns with covered face and rushes off.

The East Room broods in silence as an owl
skims over what is left of Camelot.

Visions

Hume Highway, Bookham, NSW

It was December, close to festive time.
while travelling along the crowded Hume
we saw a transport truck come thumping down
crammed with sheep, all destined for the yards,
canvas flaps strapped tightly. Watched it grind up
melting bitumen, all three trays full
in wind that blisterered, landscape scarred and brown,
roadside bright with cans and broken glass.

We passed and left the livestock far behind.
Soon enough the sheep would all be cooled.
A sickle moon was rising as we wound
through country towns. I saw the evening star
and visions of a child filled my mind—
A lamb. The need for humans to be kind.

The Passage

That momentary rush of evening light
when all is quiet. The gentle evening light.

Wattle birds whip by with soundless flight
across the light. The softly flooding light.

I sit and watch the day spin into night
In honeyed light. In silent evening light

The moon is up and sailing like a kite
to welcome night. But, first, the golden light,

for this is time to hold the moment tight,
recalling light. That long-gone evening light,

and those I loved who drifted out of sight
into the light. The healing evening light.

Shall I chant thanksgiving? Yes, I might—
for this blessed light. This gentle evening light.

Afterword

Is there any poet who would not revel in the challenge of weaving words and music into fourteen lines? Short poems make perfect performance pieces. The sonnet will always be with us because of its neat, economical framework, driving iambic feet and elements of surprise. Being fourteen lines long, well-written sonnets also make perfect performance pieces in venues where audiences are easily distracted.

In the Middle Ages, the Italian poet Francesco Petrarch (1304-1374) refined an earlier form of sonnet by Giacomo da Lentini (1220-1270). Petrarchan sonnets explored themes of courtly love where the poet could 'immortalise' his passion for some beautiful, unattainable lady.

William Shakespeare (1564-1616) is recognised for having divided the sonnet into three quatrains, closing with a powerful couplet to define the conclusion. For many years, Shakespeare's sonnets have graced the stage, both spoken and sung. In 2016, William Zappa and Tobias Cole commemorated the four hundredth anniversary of Shakespeare's death by performing all 154 sonnets in The Street Theatre, Canberra.

The curtal sonnet was invented by Gerald Manley Hopkins (1844-1889) to describe a shortened sonnet consisting of ten lines plus one half line, which is 3/4 of a Petrarchan sonnet. Hopkins' best known curtal sonnets are 'Pied Beauty' and 'Peace.'

Like free verse, contemporary sonnets tend to be unrhymed and most follow the rhythms of speech rather than iambic pentameter. Some conclude with a rhyming couplet reminiscent of a Shakespearean sonnet. This brings a freedom that I'm still exploring, like many poets before me. Sonneteers have also played with line length. The elegant Alexandrine line is written in iambic hexameter. There are only a couple of Alexandrine sonnets in this collection, but I'm very attracted to the style.

The idea of writing paired sonnets, where the second poem develops material from the first, has always attracted me (see Gwen Harwood's 'In the Park' and 'I' from *Later Texts*, in Geoff Page's *The Indigo Book of Modern Australian Sonnets (2003)*. Alternatively, sonnets might be arranged in sequences, practiced by sonneteers as early as Petrarch's time. A crown of sonnets echoes the last line of the previous sonnet in the first line of the next, with the fifteenth sonnet created from those final lines. Poets have also published longer sequences, exemplified in Ellen Bryant Voigt's *Kyrie* (1995), fifty-five sonnets exploring the Spanish Flu epidemic, Moira Egan's *Hot Flash Sonnets* (2013), a themed sequence on menopause in twenty-eight sonnets. My own small collection takes the form of a radio play.

I am fascinated by similarities between the sonnet and short Eastern poetic forms, particularly the Japanese forms of haiku and tanka (Jp. tanka : 'short song'; Ital. sonnet: 'little song'). In their traditional forms, both unfold musically. They pivot to express a new idea, similar to a volta. A tanka sequence links and shifts like a crown of sonnets. The six-line sedoka is another Japanese form with a noticeable turn in line four. However, a sonnet should not be viewed as an extended haiku, tanka, sedoka or the like. Firstly, the pivot serves a different function in shorter forms, where brevity is the essence. It may even be expressed in a single word. Secondly, most sonnets tend towards two turns: one at the beginning of the sestet, the second occurring in the final couplet. Thirdly, metre is not used in Eastern styles. Nevertheless, they must always flow musically. In this sense, haiku and tanka are more like contemporary sonnets than the older, closed sonnet forms. There are other issues, but I will not investigate them here.

I've always maintained that the spoken word is part of the vast spectrum we call song. Singing is simply another form of human expression and communication. As the distinguished musicologist George List once explained to me, only stability of intonation distinguishes song from speech. Some poems in this collection attempt to show how animals and birds communicate by creating their own 'poetry' and 'music', inspiring composers like Hooper Brewster Jones (1887-1949) and Oliver Messiaen (1908-1992) to transcribe bird songs and include them in musical works. In this tradition, 'sound poets' imbue their poems with one or two sounds, as in Elizabeth Barret Browning's 'Sonnet 43' (1806-1861).

At what point is a sonnet not a sonnet? A friend once advised me that cake recipes must be strictly followed on the first time of making. After the recipe is perfected, experimentation is permitted. I have included a ghazal in this collection, to show that it, too, can display similarities with the sonnet. Readers may further observe that some hybrids in this collection are so removed for the original form that they are scarcely recognisable. But, on close examination, remnants of the original form will remain. Most travel on iambic feet, have some change of direction, and all remain fourteen lines long.

Notes

"Hindsight", p. 10

Inspired by an old photograph, this poem explores recent concerns about the USA gun lobby. See John R. Lott. *More Guns, Less Crime: Understanding Crime and Gun Control Laws.* University of Chicago Press, 2010.

"Boundaries", p. 12

When we bought our country home in New South Wales, the back gate reminded me of my childhood. I was sad to see it go. 'Don't Fence Me In' is a popular American song, written in 1934, with music by Cole Porter and lyrics by Robert Fletcher and Cole Porter.

"The Miner's Wife", p. 16

Inspired by our travels to South Australia for further research on my husband Christopher's book *From Copper to Gold* (2014).

"Kyrie", p. 18

A response to Ellen Bryant Voight's book of sonnets based on the Spanish Flu epidemic of 1919. With thanks to Marianne Boruch and Ellen Bryant Voight for their support. See Ellen Bryant Voigt. *Kyrie.* Norton, 1995.

"The Cost", p. 19

Triggered by the Covid 19 pandemic. Double cross (golf) A score whereby a player tries for a fade and hits a hook or tries for a draw and hits a slice. Albatross (golf): A score given to a hole completed in three strokes under par.

"Dazzled", p. 29

In memory of the Australian geologist Robert Tingey, who served as Secretary of the Scientific Committee of the Antarctic Research Working Group on Geology for eight years. He was awarded the Australian Antarctic Medal in 1980. A number of geographic features in Antarctica are named after him including the Tingey Glacier in the southern Prince Charles Mountains.

"Rucksack", p. 30

This rucksack has travelled all around the world.

"The Kongouro from New Holland", p. 32

The *Kongouro* is by George Stubbs (1724-1806). It is the first painting of an Australian animal. The work was commissioned by Sir Joseph Banks who travelled with Lieutenant James Cook on his first voyage of discovery and first displayed at the National Maritime Museum, Greenwich, 1773.

"Returned Soldier, 1948", p. 33

Information for this poem came from the Sandakan families' gathering in 2012. A group of returned soldiers who were fortunate enough to miss the Death March shared their experiences with us, with stories of terrible years of shell shock and depression. I am grateful to Bill Young, who gave us a copy of a book of poems recounting his years of internment. Bill died of Covid in May, 2022. Recruited as a teenager, he was 96 years old when he passed away.

"Noh", p. 35

Noh is a stylised classical Japanese music-drama perfected by Zeami (1363-1443) where actors recreate ancient legends using elaborate costumes and masks and is believed to suspend actors and audience in a supernatural state.

"Hummingbird", p. 37

The Nazca lines are giant geoolyths created by ancient Peruvians 500 BC and 400 AD in the Nazca desert. Some of these are figures, like the humming bird, monkey, whale and astronaut.

"Message to Mama After the Airstrike", p. 39

An imagined poem based on reports of two children and their donkeys, who were killed in Afghanistan during a military operation between NATO and the Taliban in March, 2013.

https://www.nytimes.com/2013/03/03/world/asia/two-afghan-boys-accidentally-killed-by-nato-helicopter/

"Purplue Skies", p. 41

A found poem based on Keats' letters to Fanny Brawne: https://englishhistory.net/keats/letters/fanny-brawne-february-1820/

"Letter to Theo", p. 42

A poem that evolved from the gift of a book from my sister Virginia after I had seen the Van Gogh painting in New York. R. Thompson, 2008. Vincent van Gogh. *The Starry Night*. New York: Museum of Modern Art.

"On Driving down North Jindalee Road", p. 43

North Jindalee Road runs off the Olympic Highway near Cootamundra and connects to Burley Griffin Way at Wallendbeen. Due to its narrow width and uneven surface, it is seldom used by cars or trucks. This road has always been a favourite road of mine, because of its therapeutic beauty and the chance of seeing all kinds of wildlife.

"To My Widow", p. 45

An improvisation on Robert Falcon Scott's last letter to his wife Katherine, dated March, 1912. Scott Polar Research Institute Museum, Department of Geography, University of Cambridge. Titus Oates died on 16 March 1912.

"I Am Just Going Outside", p. 46

An imagined letter written at Ross Shelf, Antarctica a day before Scott's death on 29 March. The title of this poem is based on the last words of Titus Oates.

"Friesias on the Hillside", p. 49

At one end of the bail where cows were milked was a tray for feed. This enabled the cow's head to be secured with the bailing pin before milking. The cows' 'names' were still visible over the bails when the farm was sold.

"On an Unmarked Grave", p. 50

The historic Wallendbeen Cemetery holds the remains of a number of children who perished while only young. This is an imagined poem based on one of them. I was unable to find any information on the child or grave in the Cootamundra Council records. The state of this little resting place suggests that the child was born in poverty.

"Words Remembered", p. 53

Celebrates the contribution of John Saxon and Mike Dinn (Depuy Director) at Honeysuckle Creek, Namadji, ACT, on July 16, 1969 as images of the moon landing were beamed from space. Saxon was the first to see the images. The Honeysuckle team was led by Director Tom Reid. A picture appeared in *The Canberra Times* on March 17, 2017, showing Saxon with a cigarette in his hand. It was later photoshopped off the celebratory one-dollar coin for political correctness along with Armstrong's famous words on landing on the moon.

https://www.canberratimes.com.au/story/6035264/honeysuckle-creek-celebrates-50-years-of-making-space-history/

https://coinscatalog.net/australia/coin-one-dollar-50th-anniversary-moon-landing-commonwealth-of-australia-decimal-coinage/

"Carol of the Mulberry," p. 54

A Christmas carol set to the Tallis *Canon* transposed to aeolian mode. The final two lines are repeated, consistent with canonic practise. Thomas Tallis (c. 1505–1585) was an English composer whose works are still sung and celebrated today.

"Lux Benigna: Lead Kindly Light", p. 55

A lover of music, our mother chose all her funeral hymns. The text for 'Lead Kindly Light' is by John H. Newman, (1801-1890) and the setting Lux Benigna by the composer John B. Dykes (1823-1886). Although we practised this beautiful hymn diligently, nobody at the funeral knew the tune.

"Bethungra Spiral", p. 57

Historically and scientifically rare, the Bethungra Rail Spiral between Junee and Cootamundra was built in the 1940s. It is the only 360-degree spiral in Australia and one of Australia's most significant rail engineering feats of its time. The spiral is only experienced when traveling North. Stan Marks was a passionate walker who led many groups over long bush trails. He passed away shortly after riding the spiral. 'How Long Blues': https://www.youtube.com/watch?v=PqOYncRHtO8/

"A Potassium Hit's the Thing", p. 58

Many music students suffer from performance anxiety, more commonly known or 'stage fright'. This poem explores the practice of eating a banana prior to performance, creating a placebo effect that sometimes brings comfort to players.

"Let the Bass Walk with You", p. 59

Inspired by the recording *Chet Baker in Tokyo* (1987), this poem can be found on the following link: Almost Blue: https://m.youtube.com/watch?v=nxATAL9zoP8/

"Carpal Trouble," p. 60

Carpal Tunnel Syndrome (CTS) is one of several serious medical conditions which occur from overuse of the muscles used for performing. It is treated physiotherapy and surgery. CTS can be avoided by taking regular breaks during practice. A rinforzando (music) denotes a sudden increase in force.

"The Violin Maker", p. 62

I first met my husband Christopher in 1980 while taking violin lessons. The antique violin I played was a gift from my mother. Christopher had already made a contra bassoon and was inspired to craft the violin that inspired this poem.

"Another Garden", p. 64

In response to Marina Tsvetaeva's 'Sad,' with thanks to Subbash Jaireth who introduced the original poem in his translation workshop during Poetry on the Move (2017), an annual festival presented by the University of Canberra. Silvereyes are tiny Australian songbirds.

"A Hint of Rosemary", p. 65

Over the years the death of President John Kennedy has inspired many documentaries and films. This found poem is derived from an article written by Professor Daniel Metraux, who found the information in his mother's papers after her death. Nancy Tuckerman was a valued member of staff. My thanks to Professor Metraux for sharing access to that document: 'Long Lost First-Hand Report on the Kennedy Assassination Details Death Scene at the White House on 22 November 1963.' Editor's Desk. Virginia Review of Asian Studies 16, (2014), 277-288. https://virginiareviewofasianstudies.com/ First Accessed 17 November 2015.

"Visions", p. 66

Inspired by the song "All in the April Evening", from *Twenty-one Poems by Katherine Tynan: Selected by W.B. Yeats.* Dun Emer Press. Dundrum. 1907. It was set to music by Sir Hugh Robertson (1874-1952) and published by Curwen in 1911.

Publication Credits

Absence does not make the Heart Grow Fonder 'Non-human Companions,' *Burrow 3* (2021).

A Potassium Hit's the Thing, *Quadrant 63:12* (2019).

A River Crossed, *Water: Scribblers' Anthology* (2011).

Bethungra Spiral, Solicited for *MacQueen's Quinterly 15* (2022).

Big Leg, *Artsound FM* (2022).

Costco is Selling Coffins, Solicited for Judith Clingan's music theatre, *The Threshold*. Performed 4 March 2023.

Freesias on the Hillside, *Grieve* (2021).

Kongouro from New Holland, Solicited for *MacQueen's Quinterly 17* (2023).

Kyrie, *The Canberra Times Panorama* (2020).

Hard Lessons, The, *Canberra Times Panorama* (May, 2022).

Hindsight, *Artsound FM* (2023)

Hummingbird, *Sugar Loaf and Humming Birds* (2014).

Leaving Canberra, *Messages from the Embers* (2020). Solicited for *MacQueen's Quinterly 15* (2022).

Letter to Theo, *Milestones* (2021).

Makeshift Cafe, *Kokako 36* (2022).

Miner's Wife, The, *MacQueen's Quinterly 21* (2024).

Noh, *Not Very Quiet (*2021).

On a Makeshift Grave, *MacQueen's Quinterly 21* 2024.

On Driving down Jindalee Road, 'Place'. *Burrow* (2021).

Plastic Bags, *Other People Other Worlds: Scribblers' Anthology* (2011).

Purplue Skies, *Poetry d'Amour 17* (2021).

Returned Soldier, Solicited for *MacQueen's Quinterly* (2023).

Six Pigs, *Sugar Loaf and Humming Birds* (2014).

Squeezed, *Quadrant 26:9* (2022).

Words Remembered, *These Strange Outcrops* (2020).

Violin Maker, The, *Whispering Willows: Tree Poems* (2022).

Visions, *Artsound FM* (2023).

Haiku and tanka

a glimpse, *Stardust Haiku 35* (2019).
a sprig, *Presence 62*, 2026; *Moonlight over the Siding* (2018).
old mine shaft, *Blithe Spirit 32:2* (2023).
old photos, *Cattails,* April (2017).
setting sun, *Stardust Haiku 24,* (2018).
snow clouds over 'Fujisan Taisho' (2024). Hon mention.

www.ingramcontent.com/pod-product-compliance
Lightning Source LLC
Chambersburg PA
CBHW031927080426
42734CB00007B/587